W____ IS THIS JESUS?

Overwhelming Evidence for Those Who
Want to Know the Real Truth!

Bill Rudge

LIVING TRUTH PUBLISHERS
A Division of Bill Rudge Ministries, Inc.
Hermitage, Pennsylvania
www.billrudge.org

Who Is This Jesus?

Copyright © 1988 by Bill Rudge
Updated and expanded edition copyright © 2002
by Bill Rudge
ISBN 1-889809-03-9

Published by Living Truth Publishers
A Division of Bill Rudge Ministries, Inc.
Hermitage, Pennsylvania

Cover design: Jay O. Gould

Contents

I Didn't Need Jesus Christ!

I was eighteen and everything was going great. I had a beautiful girlfriend, a dream job as a weightlifting instructor, and was gaining notoriety in karate as Godzilla. No one would have been happier than me to discover that the Bible was not God's Word and Jesus Christ was not whom He claimed to be. Then I could have continued in my delusion that I was god. I could have remained lord of my self-centered lifestyle.

So Why Do I Now Follow Him?

I came to Christ not because my life was all messed up or because I thought I needed Him, but because I knew there was something missing that nothing or no one else could satisfy. The more I searched, the more aware I became that I was usurping God's rightful place in my life. Still, I didn't want to hear about it and suppressed the truth.

Almost everything imaginable was tried, even hitchhiking across the country. But my search to find what was missing was still not fulfilled. Then on May 23, 1971, at the age of eighteen, my life was dramatically changed through a personal encounter with Jesus Christ. I came to know Him as my Savior and Lord. It wasn't because I needed a crutch, but because of the compelling evidence I could not deny.

Reasons Some Believe

A man once said to me, "Bill, you are the most committed person I know. You have such strong faith that you would probably give your life for Jesus Christ." I replied, "I am so convinced that Jesus Christ is who He claims to be that I could never deny Him."

He asked me why I was so confidently committed. I explained that there are many ways in which a person comes to believe in and adhere to a religious or a philosophical belief system.

Some are forced to accept certain beliefs or else be persecuted or martyred. Many are raised in families or live in countries where they will be disowned, treated harshly, or even put to death if they do not adhere to the commonly accepted belief system.

Some, who are born and raised in a particular religious system, accept what they are taught and what everyone else believes. They do not have valid reasons for their beliefs; they simply accept what their culture has taught them.

Others are open to religious experiences as a result of a particular crisis—a divorce, loss of a job or a loved one, or other situations which make them emotionally vulnerable. They come in contact with an individual or group who befriends them and offers emotional support, or they have a *spiritual* experience which causes them to join that group and adhere to its beliefs.

I became a believer in Jesus Christ for none of these reasons, but because the truth became increasingly clear as I examined the facts. In no way did I want to give my life to the Jesus of the Bible. But as I honestly searched, I could not deny the overwhelming evidence which answered my questions. I wanted to know: Is there a God? If there is a God, are there many ways to God or only one? If there is only one way to God, what is it? How do I come to know the true God?

Of all religious books, only the Bible has conclusive evidence that it is the Word of God. Of all religious leaders, only Jesus Christ presents the undeniable proof that He is who He claimed to be. I was persuaded, not because I was forced to believe by threat of death, nor because I was raised in a Christian culture. It was not out of convenience because everyone else believed this way, and it was not because I had an emotional crisis. I became a committed believer in Jesus Christ because I was convinced He is the ultimate Truth for which I had so earnestly searched.

Jeremiah 29:13 accurately states—

You will seek Me and find Me when you search for Me with all your heart.

Rejecting the Wrong Jesus

As I spoke with a lady in Phoenix who was involved in the new age movement, I shared with her that I was a Christian. She immediately wanted to terminate the conversation because she had been repulsed by many dogmatic and narrow-minded Christians who said Jesus is the only way. When she realized that I was willing to listen and that I was not going to condemn her, she listened to me with a receptive, open mind.

I said to her, "If Jesus is not the only way of salvation, then Christians are dogmatic, but if He is, then Christians are merely being truthful." I continued, "Either the Jesus of the Bible is wrong and we are all one with the universe and divine, and there are many ways to salvation, or Jesus is right and the others are counterfeits." Just believing in something doesn't make it true, no matter how sincere you are. It is not the intensity of belief that makes something true; it is who and what you believe in that really matters.

I then shared some convincing facts about the greatest One who has ever lived—the evidence for His existence, the truthfulness of His words, the accounts of His life, and the prophecies and promises He fulfilled. What she was rejecting were false and inaccurate concepts of Christianity and

Jesus Christ, not genuine Christianity and the true Jesus of the Bible. Before ending our conversation she told me that, for the first time, the Bible and Christianity made sense. For further explanation, she requested some materials published by our ministry.

Who Do People Say Jesus Is?

We are constantly bombarded with such a variety of religious ideas and philosophies that some people do not know what to believe. We are surrounded with conflicting beliefs through the music and messages we hear, the movies we watch, the books and magazines we read, and the people we meet. Is it any wonder many cry out in despair, "Just where do I find truth?"

As I travel throughout the world, I frequently ask people, "Who is Jesus Christ?" I get a variety of answers from the many different types of people I encounter. The responses vary depending on the beliefs the person holds. They usually respond in one of the following ways:

- They say He was a good man (although some would say He was an evil man).

- They deny His deity by demoting Him to merely one of many great teachers or prophets who have come to show the way to God (Some would say He's a false prophet).

- They say He was just another "would be" Messiah who failed.

- They admit He was the perfect master of His time, but now believe someone else has replaced Him as the progressive revelation and incarnation of God.

- They say Jesus was a man in whom the Christ spirit dwelled, but now the Christ spirit is reincarnated in someone else.

- They acknowledge His deity, but rob Him of His uniqueness by elevating others or themselves to His level by saying we are all God and possess the potential to be like Him.

Many are quick to say, "Sure, Jesus is God, but you and I are also God." They reason that we all are indwelt by the Christ spirit; we all have the potential to become a Christ. When we realize we are all one and all divine, we will achieve Christ consciousness. Yet this very answer reveals their total misunderstanding of what Christ taught and whom He claimed to be.

Counterfeit Jesus

It is important to realize that there is more than one Jesus mentioned in the New Testament—the Jesus of the Bible and "another Jesus." In II Corinthians 11:3,4, the apostle Paul states—

> But I am afraid that, as the serpent deceived Eve by his craftiness, your minds will be led astray from the simplicity and purity of devotion to Christ. For if one comes and preaches another Jesus whom we have not preached...or a different gospel which you have not accepted, you bear this beautifully.

The Biblical test of a spiritual counterfeit is determined by the opinion one ultimately holds of Jesus Christ (I John 4:1-3; I John 2:22,23). It is imperative, therefore, that we know and believe in the Jesus of the Bible and not "another Jesus."

Thus it is necessary to examine, "Who is this Jesus?" The implications of this question need to be considered by everyone, for how you answer this question will determine your eternal destiny.

Come along and let me share some facts about the greatest One who has ever lived.

Messianic Prophecies

When tested by the Pharisees and Sadducees who asked for a sign from heaven, Jesus said to them—

> When it is evening, you say, "It will be fair weather, for the sky is red." And in the morning, "There will be a storm today, for the sky is red and threatening." Do you know how to discern the appearance of the sky, but cannot discern the signs of the times? (Matthew 16:2,3).

The "signs of the times" to which Jesus referred were the numerous prophecies concerning the Messiah that had been made hundreds of years before He was incarnated on earth. These were fulfilled in exact detail by only one person in history—and that person is Jesus of Nazareth.

The Fullness of Time

The apostle Paul said, "When the fullness of the time came, God sent forth His Son..." (Galatians 4:4). The "fullness of the time" means when every exact detail has been seen to and is in place so as to identify without a doubt who is God's only begotten Son. The exact details to which Paul was referring were the prophecies in the Hebrew Bible concerning the coming of the promised Messiah that described His birth, the city of His birth, His genealogy consisting of the tribe, family, and house from which He was to come, the scope of His ministry, the way He would die, and more.

Skeptics, unable to deny that Jesus fulfilled the messianic prophecies, often add that He deliberately attempted to do so. Yet, how could Jesus have humanly controlled the circumstances of His life to fulfill so many prophecies such as His ancestry, the time and location of His birth, the flight into Egypt as a child, the darkness over the land during His crucifixion, and so on?

In his exhaustive book, *All the Messianic Prophecies of the Bible*, Dr. Herbert Lockyer unfolds the more than 300 references to the Messiah in the Hebrew Scriptures that were fulfilled in Jesus of Nazareth. He also shows how the Christ is revealed symbolically in numerous Old Testament personages, historical events, religious rituals, feasts, and festivals. After convincingly presenting the proof that Jesus is the promised Messiah, Dr. Lockyer ends his book of over 500 pages by stating:

> Well, our task has been a long and arduous one, but most inspiring and rewarding, for in multitudinous ways we have discovered how wonderfully true the Master's own word is: IN THE VOLUME OF THE BOOK IT IS WRITTEN OF ME![1]

While many may claim to be the Messiah, only One has fulfilled the requirements set down in

Scripture. No one other than Jesus of Nazareth can legitimately say, "I am the promised Messiah." No one else can meet the Biblical criteria.

Genealogical Records Destroyed

Concerning the Messiah's credentials, Fred John Meldau writes in *Messiah in Both Testaments*:

> Jesus of Nazareth fulfills ALL the specifications as to His lineage, His birthplace, and the time of His birth. And is it not most remarkable that within a generation of Christ's sufferings on the cross the temple was destroyed, the Jewish priesthood ceased to exist, the sacrifices were no longer offered, the Jews' genealogical records were destroyed, their city was destroyed, and the people of Israel were driven out of their land, sold into slavery, and dispersed to the four corners of the earth! Since those dreadful national judgments fell on Israel it has been utterly impossible for a "Messiah" to come with proper "credentials," such as the Old Testament demands, and such as Jesus of Nazareth presented.[2]

Meldau also points out:

> During Bible times, every Jew could trace his genealogy. "So all Israel were reckoned by genealogies" (I Chronicles 9:1). These records were kept in the cities (Nehemiah 7:5,6; Ezra 2:1) and were public property. Each Israelite's genealogical record constituted his title to his farm or home—so he had a pecuniary interest in preserving the genealogical records of his family. These national genealogical records

were carefully kept until the destruction of Jerusalem and the temple and the Jewish state in 70 A.D. During the life of Jesus, no one offered to dispute the well known fact that He was of the house and lineage of David, because it was in the public records that all had access to.

Since 70 A.D., when Israel's genealogical records, except those in the Bible, were destroyed or confused, no pretending Messiah can prove he is the son of David as prophecy demands. In other words, Messiah had to come before 70 A.D.[3]

Daniel's Prophecy of the Seventy Weeks

Insight concerning Daniel's amazing prophecy about the seventy weeks is given in *The Search for Messiah*. Excerpts follow:

The prophecy states that "seventy sevens" are determined for the people of Israel. In Hebrew the word translated as "sevens" is the plural form of the word "shabua"...which literally means a week of years; much like the English word decade means ten years.

The prophecy declares that Daniel should "know and understand" that from the going forth of the command to restore and rebuild Jerusalem, until the Messiah the Prince comes, that there will be sixty-two sevens and seven sevens of years. Therefore, if a seven (shabua) is seven years, then 69 sevens is 483 years (69 x 7 = 483 years).

...The prophecy then states that after the Messiah is "cut off," the people of the prince who is to come would "destroy the city and the sanctuary." In the year 70 C.E., ten legions of Roman soldiers under the Roman general Titus Vespasian destroyed the city of Jerusalem and the Second Temple. Josephus dramatically records that the city was burned to the ground and millions of Jews were killed, cannibalized or starved to death.

A final note on this prophecy. It was written by Daniel at a time when the temple in Jerusalem was desolate. Destroyed in 587 B.C.E., there was no indication in Daniel's day that it would be rebuilt. However, Daniel states that after the temple was rebuilt, the Messiah would come and then "the prince of the people who is to come" would destroy it again. So the Messiah had to come to the Second Temple before it was destroyed! In the aftermath of the Roman invasion the people wept in the streets, crying that the temple had been destroyed yet Messiah had not come.[4]

Rachmiel Frydland was a Jewish man who suffered through the Nazi invasion of Poland and escaped to tell his story of how he came to know Yeshua (Jesus) as the Messiah. He had an extensive knowledge of Jewish Scripture and rabbinic writings. In his book, *What the Rabbis Know About the Messiah*, Rachmiel Frydland writes:

The study of our greatest sages brought them to the conclusion that if the dates in the Scriptures are correct, then Messiah should have come in the first century of our era, or thereabouts.

...We may ask: Why was He expected during the first century? Clearly there was a certainty that Messiah had to appear at that period. This conviction was probably based upon the following passages in the book of Daniel:

Seventy weeks (or heptads— weeks of years) are determined upon the people and upon the Holy City, to finish the transgression, and to make an end of sins, and to make reconciliation for iniquity, and to bring in everlasting righteousness, and to seal up the vision and prophecy, and to anoint the most Holy. Know, therefore, and understand that from the going forth of the commandment to restore and to rebuild Jerusalem unto the Messiah, the Prince, shall be seven weeks, and three score and two weeks; the street shall be built again; and the wall, even in troublous times. And after threescore and two weeks shall Messiah be cut off, but not for himself: and the people of the prince that shall come shall destroy the city and the sanctuary, and the end of it shall be with a flood, and unto the end of the war desolations are determined (Daniel 9:24-26).

This revelation was a result of Daniel's prayers given to him by the angel Gabriel to explain the time, substance and circumstance of Israel's redemption.

The time embraced was "seventy sevens." Within the sixty-nine heptads (weeks of years), that is within 483 years, there will be a building up of Jerusalem's streets and canals, though in troublous times. After these 483 years, "Messiah will be cut off and not for himself." After Messiah is cut off, the city of Jerusalem and the Holy Temple will be destroyed "by the people of the prince that shall come." Messiah was to come before the destruction of the Temple. This is the picture that the archangel Gabriel gave to Daniel.[5]

Frydland continues:

It was Daniel's prophecy that challenged me many years ago to consider the Messiahship of Yeshua the Nazarene. Rabbinic authorities to whom I consulted said that the reference to Messiah in Daniel's prophecy was to King Agrippa, Herod's descendant, who is called "Messiah" here and who was "cut off" before the Temple's destruction. Hence, the term "Messiah" is transferred to a carnal king, like Agrippa, or to the unknown Menachem Ben Amiel as recorded in the Midrash. On the other hand, I learned of Yeshua the Nazarene, who was "cut off" forty years before the Second Temple was destroyed.

The revelation given to Daniel also deals with the substance and the circumstances of Messiah's activity, "to finish the transgression, to make an end of sins and to make reconciliation for iniquity and to bring in everlasting righteousness." In other words, Messiah's death is distinctly connected with the atoning work that the Temple sacrifices were to accomplish, except that it would be a work of completion and fulfillment far greater than any Temple sacrifices could possibly secure. I was thus enabled to lay aside my fears and prejudices and to open the *Brit Hadasha* [New Testament] and learn more of him, who, as the Prophet says:

Hath borne our griefs and carried our sorrows; yet we did esteem Him stricken, smitten of God and afflicted. But He was pierced through for our transgressions, He was bruised for our iniquities, the chastisement for our peace was upon him, and with his stripes we are healed (Isaiah 53:4,5).

Yeshua indeed fits perfectly into Daniel's timetable. No one else qualifies; neither King Agrippa nor the mystical Menachem fulfills Daniel's prophecy. Yeshua is the Messiah! He came to give peace to the individual who repents and accepts his atoning sacrifice. He is coming again in might to establish his Kingdom....[6]

Contradictions Resolved

There are three apparent contradictions concerning the Messiah that seem to be impossible to resolve. A prophecy found in Micah 5:2 in the Tanakh (Old Testament) states (seven centuries before the event) that Bethlehem was to be the birthplace of the Messiah. However, we also read that God would call His son out of Egypt (Hosea 11:1— initially referring to Israel, but ultimately fulfilled in Jesus). To make matters more complicated, it had been spoken by the prophets that He would be a Nazarene.

This dilemma is resolved in the person of Jesus of Nazareth. Caesar Augustus issued a decree that a census should be taken of the entire Roman world. Since Joseph and Mary belonged to the house and lineage of David, they were required to leave Nazareth and travel to their family's town of origin, Bethlehem of Judea. It was during their short time in Bethlehem that Jesus was born (Luke 2:1-7). Then, as a child, He was taken by His parents to Egypt to flee Herod's massacre (Matthew 2:13-18). After the crisis was past, He was called out of Egypt (Matthew 2:19-21) and was raised in His parents' hometown of Nazareth, thus being called a Nazarene (Matthew 2:23).

Interwoven Throughout Scripture

The messianic prophecies are interwoven throughout the Hebrew Scriptures. A partial list follows which was excerpted from a messianic magazine:

He was to be of the seed of the woman (Genesis 3:15; Galatians 4:4), of Abraham (Genesis 22:18; Galatians 3:16), of Judah (Genesis 49:10; Hebrews 7:14), and then of David (2 Samuel 7:12,13; Jeremiah 23:5; Acts 13:23). The Deliverer was to be born at a certain time (Daniel 9:24-27) in a designated city (Micah 5:2; Luke 2:4-7); and His birth was to be preceded by the ministry of a forerunner (Isaiah 40:3; Malachi 3:1; Matthew 3:1-3).

His ministry was to commence in Galilee (Isaiah 9:1,2; Matthew 4:12-17,23), but He was also to enter Jerusalem (Zechariah 9:9; Matthew 21:1-5) where He would possess the Temple (Malachi 3:1; Mark 11:15-18). The Messiah's ministry was to be punctuated with miracles (Isaiah 35:5,6; Luke 7:21,22); yet He would be despised (Isaiah 49:7; John 7:48; 15:25), rejected by the nation's rulers (Psalm 118:22; Matthew 21:42), betrayed by someone close to Him (Psalm 41:9; John 13:18-22), and abandoned for 30 pieces of silver (Zechariah 11:13; Matthew 26:15).

He would be smitten on the cheek (Micah 5:1; Matthew 27:30), spat on (Isaiah 50:6; Matthew 27:30), mocked (Psalm 22:7,8;

Matthew 27:31, 39-44), and scourged (Isaiah 50:6; Matthew 27:26-30), yet none of His bones would be broken (Psalm 34:20; John 19:33-36). His body was to be buried with the wealthy (Isaiah 53:9; Matthew 27:57-60) but was to remain uncorrupted (Psalm 16:10; Acts 2:31) because, shortly after dying, He would rise miraculously from the grave (Psalm 2:7; 16:10; Acts 13:33). [7]

All these prophecies, and many more, were fulfilled in the person of Jesus of Nazareth—not one of which is inconsistent with the history of His life.

Prophecies in Psalm 22

Psalm 22 is inseparably associated with the crucifixion, not only because the opening words were quoted by Jesus, but because much of the Psalm accurately describes His body condition and emotional experience.

Concerning Psalm 22, *The Eerdmans Bible Commentary* states:

> The details of Calvary are all so clearly here; mockery (v.8), shame (vv. 13,17), the pain of crucifixion (vv. 14-16)—for even if 'pierced' (v. 16) is an uncertain translation (*cf.* mg.), the agony to hands and feet is specifically mentioned—and the parting of garments (v. 18). All this took place by the agency of those [Romans] who neither knew the Scriptures nor had any interest in fulfilling them, and provides dramatic and unanswerable evidence of the divine inspiration of the Bible and of the faithfulness of God to His Word.[8]

David, who had never seen or heard of such a method of execution, gave a graphic portrayal of death by crucifixion in Psalm 22. Even more interesting is the fact that this was recorded one thousand years before the time of Christ, and hundreds of years before crucifixion ever existed as a form of capital punishment.

The usual Jewish method of execution was stoning, but God in His unique way arranged it so that Rome would be in control to fulfill David's prophecy concerning the crucifixion. If the Jewish leaders would have had their way, they would have stoned Jesus, but in fulfillment of Scripture, He was crucified.

From Servant to King

Although written 700 years before the time of Jesus, Isaiah 53 is a vivid description of the Messiah's death as a substitutionary sacrifice. Concerning Isaiah 53, scholar and commentator Adam Clarke states:

> That this chapter speaks of none but Jesus must be evident to every unprejudiced reader who has ever heard the history of His sufferings and death.[9]

The Search for Messiah, in which numerous ancient Jewish sources and rabbis were quoted, states:

> The evidence speaks for itself. Throughout most of the history of Jewish scholarship many of the highly respected writers of the Talmud and the Midrash (most of whom were leaders of rabbinical academies) shared a common belief.

The Messiah would be despised, rejected, suffer by being pierced and ultimately die for the sins of the people.[10]

The *Wycliffe Bible Dictionary* sheds additional light concerning the Messiah:

> Isaiah introduces another stream into the river of messianic prophecy in the Servant of the Lord passages (42:1-9; 49:1-6; 50:4-9; 52:13-53:12) which find their culmination in Isaiah 53. Here the Servant of the Lord is a rejected, suffering leader who dies a substitutionary death for His people and yet prolongs His days and prospers.
>
> Daniel provides yet another tributary to this swelling stream as he tells of his visions of the end time. In a crucial vision he sees a figure "like the Son of man" coming on the clouds of heaven and receiving from the Ancient of Days a glorious, universal, everlasting, and final kingdom (Daniel 7:13). The vision contains the paradoxical elements of humanity and deity in the phrases "like the Son of man" and "coming on the clouds of heaven," since Son of man means human being, and the clouds of heaven were considered to be the vehicle of God.
>
> ...it is evident that this rich and varied presentation of one who was to come to usher in the day of the Lord issued in the notion of different Messiahs. Not before Jesus of Nazareth guided these tributaries into one stream did anyone find it possible to harmonize in one person all the messianic hopes.
>
> ...Many of these prophecies are declared by the NT writers to be fulfilled in Jesus' first

advent. Others are by Jesus Himself related to the current period between the two advents or to the time of His return; if not for their initial fulfillment, certainly for their culmination.[11]

Will Messiah Come Twice?

The Search for Messiah points out:

During our examination of messianic prophecy we found that there were "two veins" of prophecy recognized by the ancient rabbis regarding the life, ministry and destiny of the Messiah. Several prophecies predicted a suffering servant who would die for the sins of the people while others predicted a ruling and reigning Messiah.

...Jewish scholars of ancient and modern times have had great difficulty in uniting these two "veins" of prophecy in the life of a single individual. Therefore, early in rabbinical Judaism, we saw that the Messiah was split into two distinct personalities: Messiah Ben Joseph, the suffering servant, and Messiah Ben David, the ruling and reigning Messiah.

... Truly, Jesus' qualifications for the title Messiah are compatible with ancient rabbinical beliefs as well as the scriptures we have examined. The problem of the two "veins" of prophecy are solved when we realize that both missions are achievable by two appearances of one individual. His first appearance would be characterized by humility and suffering, his second appearance in glory and majesty.

Jesus of Nazareth is the only person in history who can bridge this gap and solve this puzzle.

The Messiah will come TWICE![12]

Prophet, Priest, and King

Jesus Christ is actually a name and a title. The name Jesus *(Iesous)* is the Greek form of the Hebrew word Joshua *(Yeshua)* meaning "Yahweh is salvation." The title Christ is derived from the Greek word *(Christos)* for Messiah (or the Hebrew *Mashiach)*. The term "Messiah" is derived from Psalm 2:2 and Daniel 9:25,26 where *Mashiach* (Hebrew)—*Messias* (Greek) means "Anointed One." The term took its meaning from the Jewish practice of "anointing" prophets, priests, and kings to their respective offices.

However, there was one unique individual to whom the term "Messiah" applied in a special sense. He would be the reality and ultimate fulfillment to which all other usages of the term "Messiah" would be but foreshadows.

Prophets, priests, and kings in the ancient Hebrew Scriptures were consecrated to office by an anointing with oil (prophets–I Kings 19:16, priests–Leviticus 8:12, kings–I Samuel 10:1).

As prophet, the coming Messiah would be "like Moses."

Deuteronomy 18:15—

The Lord your God will raise up for you a prophet like me from among you, from your countrymen, you shall listen to him.

John 6:14—

Therefore when the people saw the sign which He [Yeshua] had performed, they said, "This is truly the Prophet who is to come into the world."

As priest, Messiah is represented by Melchizedek.

Psalm 110:4—

The Lord has sworn and will not change His mind, "You are a priest forever according to the order of Melchizedek."

Hebrews 5:5,6—

So also Christ did not glorify Himself so as to become a high priest, but He who said to Him, "You are My Son, today I have begotten You;" just as He says also in another passage, "You are a priest forever according to the order of Melchizedek."

As king, Messiah is represented by King David when at His Second Coming He will reign as King of kings and Lord of lords.

Jeremiah 23:5—

"Behold, the days are coming," declares the Lord, "When I will raise up for David a righteous Branch; and He will reign as king and act wisely and do justice and righteousness in the land."

Revelation 19:16—

And on His robe and on His thigh He has a name written, "KING OF KINGS, AND LORD OF LORDS."

The *New International Dictionary of Old Testament Theology and Exegesis* states:

Once the NT [New Testament] identified Jesus as the Anointed One, the Messiah, all the unqualified references to the "anointed one" in the OT [Old Testament] could be seen to have even more relevance....The Lord has indeed selected one who is Prophet, Priest, and King. He has chosen and empowered him to fulfill what all the preceding anointed priests and prophets could never do—bring in the kingdom of God.[13]

Jesus Fulfilled Messianic Prophecy

The ancient Scriptures clearly reveal that salvation is through the Jewish Messiah. Therefore, it is imperative that through fulfillment of messianic prophecies we discover who the Messiah is. After thoroughly examining the evidence (only a small portion of which is covered in this book) I am convinced that Jesus of Nazareth is the promised Jewish Messiah.

The Holy Spirit revealed to Simeon, a devout Jew, that he would not die before he would see the Lord's Christ (Luke 2:25,26). Upon seeing the child Jesus at the Temple in Jerusalem, Simeon took Him in his arms and blessed God saying—

> Now Lord, You are releasing Your bond-servant to depart in peace, According to Your word; For my eyes have seen Your salvation, which You have prepared in the presence of all peoples (Luke 2:29-31).

While walking to the village of Emmaus, about seven miles from Jerusalem, two disciples were discussing the events which had recently taken place in Jerusalem. As they talked, Jesus approached and walked with them. The resurrected Christ said to them—

> "O foolish men and slow of heart to believe in all that the prophets have spoken! Was it not

necessary for the Christ to suffer these things and to enter into His glory?" Then beginning with Moses and with all the prophets, He explained to them the things concerning Himself in all the Scriptures (Luke 24:25-27).

After Jesus vanished the two disciples said to one another—

Were not our hearts burning within us while He was speaking to us on the road, while He was explaining the Scriptures to us? (Luke 24:32).

In Luke 24:44-48, we read of another appearance of the resurrected Christ to several disciples in Jerusalem who were initially frightened, but then were amazed and overjoyed—

Now He said to them, "These are My words which I spoke to you while I was still with you, that all things which are written about Me in the Law of Moses and the Prophets and the Psalms must be fulfilled." Then He opened their minds to understand the Scriptures, and He said to them, "Thus it is written, that the Christ would suffer and rise again from the dead the third day, and that repentance for forgiveness of sins would be proclaimed in His name to all the nations, beginning from Jerusalem. You are witnesses of these things."

Both Peter and Paul repeatedly explained to their Jewish brethren that Jesus fulfilled messianic prophecy. In Acts 3:17-24, Peter tells the Jews—

And now, brethren, I know that you acted in ignorance, just as your rulers did also. But the things which God announced beforehand by the mouth of all the prophets, that His Christ would suffer, He has thus fulfilled. Therefore repent and return, so that your sins may be wiped away, in order that times of refreshing may come from the presence of the Lord; and that He may send Jesus, the Christ appointed for you, whom heaven must receive until the period of restoration of all things about which God spoke by the mouth of His holy prophets from ancient time....And likewise, all the prophets who have spoken, from Samuel and his successors onward, also announced these days.

Acts 17:2,3—

And according to Paul's custom, he went to them, and for three Sabbaths reasoned with them from the Scriptures, explaining and giving evidence that the Christ had to suffer and rise again from the dead, and saying, "This Jesus whom I am proclaiming to you is the Christ."

Dr. Robert Morey, scholar and author, points out:

The apologetic of the early Church was powerful because it presented Jesus as the *fulfillment* of all the messianic prophecies, hopes, and longings of the Jewish people. The Christians pointed to the birth, life, teachings, death and resurrection of Jesus as the fulfillment of the description of the Messiah found in the Old Testament (I Corinthians 15:3-4).[14]

The apostle Paul stood in the audience chamber of Herod the Great's Caesarean palace before Governor Festus, King Agrippa (considered an authority on the Jewish religion), and prominent men of the city. He boldly declared that the Jewish hope and the Christian message are inseparably related—

> So, having obtained help from God, I stand to this day testifying both to small and great, stating nothing but what the Prophets and Moses said was going to take place; that the Christ was to suffer, and that by reason of His resurrection from the dead He would be the first to proclaim light both to the Jewish people and to the Gentiles (Acts 26:22,23).

In their fascinating book, *The Search for Messiah,* authors Mark Eastman and Chuck Smith comment:

> In this book we have examined only a small number of the hundreds of messianic prophecies in the Tanakh. Nevertheless, we have been able to extract a fairly complete portrait of the Messiah's character, lineage, mission and destiny according to the ancient rabbis. We have found a number of very specific requirements that any Messianic candidate must fulfill in order to be taken seriously. And we have been able to support this portrait with the writings of ancient rabbis, men who were among the most respected teachers of their time. We will refer to this scripturally established portrait as the "biblical view."
> We have seen that various rabbis of the last 2300 years believed the Messiah was an eternal

being who would be the Son of God, born of a virgin, a miracle worker of the line of David, in the city of Bethlehem. Yet he would be mocked, despised and rejected. He would have his hands and feet pierced and die for the sins of the people. And we have found evidence from the Bible that the Messiah would be a physical manifestation of God.

According to the Tanakh, the Messiah was to come to the Second Temple and after his coming, that very same temple would be destroyed. After the Second Temple was destroyed, we find a number of rabbis expressing their dismay that the Messiah had not come! They attribute this failure to the sins of the nation of Israel.

Is our biblical portrait of Messiah fulfilled in Jesus? The answer, according to the people who were eyewitnesses to his life, the people who were willing to suffer horribly for their faith is an unequivocal yes! Jesus of Nazareth fulfilled the biblical view of the Messiah! [15]

Is There Only One Way to Salvation?

While working out at the YMCA in San Diego I overheard two businessmen discussing death. One said, "I am not sure what's beyond the grave, but no one will immortalize me anyway, or remember me years from now." The other man said, "I figure whatever is out there will have to accept me as I am." I said, "I don't mean to jump in, but don't you think eternity is a long time? Therefore, it might be wise to spend a little more time considering its implications. Besides, if there is a God who created us and this universe, are you going to say to Him, 'You must accept me on my terms'?" Their look affirmed that I was relating, so I continued. "No, if there is a creator, then I want to come to Him on His terms, not mine."

They listened intently and their body language indicated they agreed with what I said so far, so I shared how I had rejected Christianity and spent many years searching in atheism, occultism, Eastern disciplines, and new ageism until my search for truth brought me back to the God of the Bible. The one guy asked, "Then Jesus Christ is the only way?" I said, "Without a doubt, because He alone has the overwhelming evidence to validate His claims." After sharing some of the evidence for the inspiration of the Bible and the claims of Christ, I thanked them for listening and they thanked me for sharing.

Jesus did not say, "I have come to share some spiritual light with you." He said, "I am the Light of the world; he who follows Me will not walk in the darkness..." (John 8:12). Jesus did not tell us just to be sincere in our beliefs. He said, "...unless you believe that I am He, you will die in your sins" (John 8:24). Jesus did not merely promise us that through Him we would overcome death. He exemplified it by rising bodily from the grave.

Jesus did not say, "Please allow Me to show you one of many ways to God." He said, "No one comes to the Father but through Me" (John 14:6). Jesus asserted that He alone is the controller of man's destiny—the One on whom our future of heaven or hell depends. If His claims are false, so are His promises of eternal life. But if they are true, then where we will spend eternity depends on whether we accept or reject Him. I John 5:11,12 states—

> And the testimony is this, that God has given us eternal life, and this life is in His Son. He who has the Son has the life; he who does not have the Son of God does not have the life.

When Jesus hung on the cross, He said, "It is finished!" God's plan of salvation was fulfilled as II Corinthians 5:19 points out, "...God was in Christ reconciling the world to Himself...." Scripture reveals the finality and uniqueness of Christ's sacrificial death. I Peter 3:18 says, "For Christ also died for sins once for all...."

Hebrews 10:10,12 indicates—

...We have been sanctified through the offering of the body of Jesus Christ once for all. But He, having offered one sacrifice for sins for all time, sat down at the right hand of God.

We have no need for any new age messiah, avatar, or further incarnations of the Christ spirit. The following Scriptures emphatically reveal that salvation is in Christ alone.

John 3:18—

He who believes in Him is not judged; he who does not believe has been judged already, because he has not believed in the name of the only begotten Son of God.

John 14:6—

Jesus said to him, "I am the way, and the truth, and the life; no one comes to the Father but through Me."

Acts 4:12—

And there is salvation in no one else; for there is no other name under heaven that has been given among men by which we must be saved.

I Timothy 2:5—

For there is one God, and one mediator also between God and men, the man Christ Jesus.

Is Jesus God?

Jesus asked His disciples 2,000 years ago—

> "Who do people say that the Son of Man is?"
> And they said, "Some say John the Baptist; and
> others, Elijah; but still others, Jeremiah, or
> one of the prophets." He said to them, "But who
> do you say that I am?" Simon Peter answered,
> "You are the Christ, the Son of the living God."
> And Jesus said to him, "Blessed are you, Simon
> Barjona, because flesh and blood did not reveal
> this to you, but My Father who is in heaven"
> (Matthew 16:13-17).

An insightful book, *Answers To Tough
Questions,* makes known some of the unique
claims of Jesus Christ:

> Among the religious leaders who have
> attained a large following throughout history,
> Jesus Christ is unique in the fact that He alone
> claimed to be God in human flesh. A common
> misconception is that some or many of the
> leaders of the world's religions made similar
> claims, but this is simply not the case.
> Buddha did not claim to be God; Moses
> never said that he was Yahweh; Mohammed did

not identify himself as Allah; and nowhere will you find Zoroaster claiming to be Ahura Mazda. Yet Jesus, the carpenter from Nazareth, said that he who has seen Him (Jesus) has seen the Father (John 14:9)....

He said that He existed before Abraham (John 8:58), and that He was equal with the Father (John 5:17,18)....

The united testimony of Jesus and the writers of the New Testament is that He was more than mere man; He was God.[16]

The Uniqueness of His Nature

The glory of Christ begins to unfold as we contemplate the mystery of His personhood:

> For a correct comprehension of the Person of Messiah, it is necessary to understand that He has a DUAL NATURE, but is a single personality: He is very God and perfect man...He is the God-man, God and man in one, indivisible personality. His humanity is seen in such names and titles as Son of Man, Son of David, Son of Abraham, etc. His Deity is seen in such names and titles as Son of God, God, Lord,...El, Elohim, etc. [17]

Concerning Christ being our mediator, Dr. Robert Morey comments:

> Christ's humanity is as essential for our salvation as is His deity (Hebrews 2:17). A Mediator between God and man who is not fully God or not fully man is like a bridge broke at either end. In order to represent us to the Father, He must be truly man. In order to represent the

Father to us, He must be truly God. A Mediator who is not quite God or not quite man is not
capable of bringing the two together.[18]

Jesus in the Hebrew Scriptures

In the Tanakh (Old Testament), we discover
many descriptions of God which either Jesus
Christ used as His own (in the four Gospels) or
which were attributed to Him by various New
Testament writers. The following comparative
descriptions help establish His true identity:

- In Genesis 1:1, we are told that God created
  the heavens and the earth. Various books of
  the New Testament reveal that Jesus Christ
  was involved in the creation of all things (John
  1:3; Colossians 1:15-17; Hebrews 1:10).

- Deuteronomy 10:17 says, "For the Lord your
  God is...the Lord of lords...." Jesus Christ is
  revealed as the "Lord of lords" in the New
  Testament (I Timothy 6:14,15; Revelation
  17:14 and 19:16).

- In Isaiah 44:6, God states, " I am the first
  and I am the last...." These same words are
  used by, and in reference to, Jesus Christ in
  Revelation 1:17; 2:8; and 22:13.

These alone are good indicators for the deity of
Jesus Christ, yet the Scriptural documentation
gets even stronger as we continue.

Jesus Claimed to Be Greater

Jesus claimed to be "greater than the temple"
(Matthew 12:6), "greater than Jonah [the prophet]"
(Matthew 12:41), and "greater than Solomon"

(Matthew 12:42). His comments indicated He was greater than Jacob (John 4:7-14), greater than Abraham (John 8:52-59), and greater than the Law (Matthew 5:21-44). Jesus also said that, "the Son of Man is Lord of the Sabbath" (Matthew 12:8).

How could any man in the Jewish culture of Jesus' day claim to be greater than the Temple, the Sabbath, the Law, the patriarchs, and the prophets? These are claims and statements Jesus could not have legitimately made unless He was, in fact, God incarnate.

Divine Attributes and Actions

Throughout His life and ministry, Jesus did and said things only God could do and say. He forgave sins (Matthew 9:6; Mark 2:5). He indicated that He had the power to give eternal life (John 17:1-3). He said that He would judge the world (John 5:22,27). He also claimed equal honor with the Father (John 5:23).

Before His ascension, Jesus revealed His omnipotence by declaring that, "All authority has been given to Me in heaven and on earth" (Matthew 28:18). He also claimed the divine attributes of omnipresence (Matthew 18:20 and 28:20) and omniscience (Revelation 2:23).

When Cornelius fell at Peter's feet and worshiped him, Peter raised him up saying, "Stand up; I too am just a man" (Acts 10:25,26). When John fell at the feet of an angel to worship him, the angel told him not to do it, but to worship God (Revelation 19:10; 22:8,9). During His temptation by Satan, Jesus said, "It is written, 'You shall worship the Lord your God, and serve Him only' " (Matthew 4:10). Yet, Jesus never stopped or rebuked anyone for worshiping Him.

Jesus accepted worship from a people who had been taught to worship God alone (Matthew 14:33; 28:9; John 9:38). Even as a child, the wise men fell down and worshiped Him (Matthew 2:2,11).

Dr. Morey gives the following insight regarding the worship of Jesus:

> Was Jesus worshiped in the New Testament? Yes. How? By the prayers and praises of the saints and by their placing their ultimate faith, hope, love, and obedience in Him. Once again, I John 1:3 becomes significant:
>
> > what we have seen and heard we proclaim to you also, that you also may have fellowship with us; and indeed *our fellowship is with the Father, and with His Son Jesus Christ.*
>
> The *substance* of our fellowship with the Son of God reveals His deity as well as His personhood. *How* do we fellowship with the Son? By talking to Him in our prayers; by extolling Him in our worship; by listening to His Word; by obeying His law; by giving Him our ultimate faith, hope, love, trust, confidence, and praise; by honoring Him as our Creator and Sovereign Lord, etc. If the Son is not deity, then our fellowshipping with Him would be the grossest kind of idolatry.[19]

When Thomas addressed the resurrected Christ as his Lord and God, Jesus did not rebuke Thomas' adoration, but only his lack of faith (John 20:28,29).

Nelson's Illustrated Encyclopedia of Bible Facts states:

There is much scriptural proof that Jesus is divine. Scripture states that there is only one God and no lesser gods (*cf.* Exodus 20:3-5; Isaiah 42:8; 44:6), yet it clearly affirms that Jesus is God (e.g., John 1:1; Romans 9:5; Hebrews 1:8). The Bible reports that Jesus was worshiped at God's command (Hebrews 1:6), while lesser spiritual beings refuse to be worshiped (Revelation 22:8,9) because worship was to be rendered only to God. Only the divine Creator may be worshiped by His creatures. But Jesus Christ, God's Son, is co-creator with His Father (John 1:3; Colossians 1:16; Hebrews 1:2); therefore both must be worshiped. Again, Scripture declares that Jesus was the Savior of His people (Matthew 1:21), even though Jehovah was the only Savior of His people (Isaiah 43:11; Hosea 13:4). It states that the Father Himself has clearly called Jesus God (Hebrews 1:8).[20]

The Theophanies

Dr. Morey writes concerning theophanies:

The word "theophany" comes from two Greek words...which simply mean *the appearance of God in human form.* These appearances were brief periods of time during which the one true God came to earth in the form of a man.

As a man, God walked, talked, ate and fellowshipped with other men. During these times, God could be seen by the human eye, touched by the human hand, and heard by the human ear. God was literally manifested in the flesh and dwelt among us. The Invisible became Visible and the Immaterial became Material without ceasing at any time to be true deity.

If it is true that God took upon Himself human form in the Old Testament, this would prepare the way for the Incarnation of the Son of God in the New Testament....

In Jesus, we are clearly confronted with The Theophany of all theophanies. But, whereas in the Old Testament, the "form of Yahweh"...was only a temporary physical manifestation, Jesus is the permanent physical manifestation of God in human form.[21]

Jesus Claimed to Be God

A casual reading of the Gospels reveals that Jesus was clear about His identity as the true God-man. Jesus said, "I and the Father are one" (John 10:30), and "He who has seen Me has seen the Father" (John 14:9). Jesus' remark in John 8:58, "Before Abraham was born, I am," caused the Jews to want to stone Him (John 8:59), because in effect He had declared Himself to be the great "I AM," which God had used to reveal Himself to Moses at the burning bush (Exodus 3:14). They realized that He was claiming to be God. (See also John 5:17,18 and 10:31-33.)

Jesus unmistakably claimed to be God in human form, although He had relinquished some of His preincarnate glory (John 17:5). Even many of the most monotheistic (those who believe in only one God) people in Jesus' day (the Jews) were finally convinced that He was God in human flesh. Jesus could have much more easily convinced the Romans, the Egyptians, or the Greeks who believed in many gods. Instead, He revealed Himself to a people who were convinced there is only one God. In the cultural setting in which He lived, there could be no misunderstanding. Jesus was not teaching that we all are divine. He was claiming to be uniquely God, manifest in human form. Numerous Old and New Testament Scriptures affirm the deity of Christ. (See Isaiah 9:6; Matthew 1:23; John 1:1,14,18; Philippians 2:5,6; Colossians 2:9; Titus 2:13; Hebrews 1:8; and II Peter 1:1.)

In Revelation 1:8, Jesus is described as "the Almighty." Concerning this, *The New International Dictionary of New Testament Theology* says:

> The term *pantokrator*, the Almighty, the Lord of all, occurs both in connection with OT quotations (II Corinthians 6:18; cf. Hosea 1:10; Isaiah 43:6) and independently (Revelation 1:8; 4:8; 11:17; 15:3; 16:7,14; 19:6,15; 21:22). In both cases the title serves to describe the immense greatness of God. He has power over all men and all things.[22]

In imagery suggestive of the countless multitude before the "Ancient of Days" as indicated in Daniel 7:10, we read in Revelation 5:11-14 of all creation giving praise to Jesus Christ—

> Then I looked, and I heard the voice of many angels around the throne and the living creatures and the elders; and the number of them was myriads of myriads, and thousands of thousands, saying with a loud voice, "Worthy is the Lamb that was slain to receive power and riches and wisdom and might and honor and glory and blessing." And every created thing which is in heaven and on the earth and under the earth and on the sea, and all things in them, I heard saying, "To Him who sits on the throne,

and to the Lamb, be blessing and honor and glory and dominion forever and ever." And the four living creatures kept saying, "Amen." And the elders fell down and worshiped.

Scripture clearly reveals that Jesus Christ is God incarnate and worthy to be worshiped.

Liar, Lunatic, or Lord?

Once we realize that Jesus claimed to be God, there are only three alternatives. As stated by many others, Jesus is either a liar, a lunatic, or Lord. Before we briefly examine each, let us lay to rest the erroneous concept that Jesus was merely a legend who never existed.

Just a Legend?

If Jesus was just a legend, then considering claims attributed to Him is a waste of time. However, the facts of history speak for themselves:

> A person today would have to commit intellectual suicide to deny the historicity of Jesus Christ. There are a multitude of non-Biblical historians, contemporaries of Jesus, who wrote and alluded to His life and death. Tacitus, Josephus, Thallus, Lucian, Seutonius, Pliny the Younger, Tertullian, and many more wrote of this man of Galilee....Our very calendar, the fact that all history is divided at the birth of Christ, bears witness to His having lived. A person would have to deny all of human history to say that Jesus is just legend.[23]

Was Jesus a Liar?

If Jesus made His claims when He knew He was not God, then He was a liar. He also was a hypocrite, because He taught others to be truthful and spoke out against hypocrisy. Worse yet, He would have been extremely evil because He told others to trust Him with their eternal destiny. Finally, He was a fool, for it was His claim to being God that led to His crucifixion (Mark 14:61-64; John 19:7).

The idea of Jesus being a liar seems ridiculous in light of His unblemished character and high moral teachings. His enemies had to hire false witnesses to testify against Him. When their fabricated evidence was discredited, Pilate asked them, "Why do you want Him to be crucified? What evil has He done?" After carefully examining their trumped-up charges, Pilate again exclaimed, "I find no fault in Him!" Even Judas, who betrayed Him for monetary gain, confessed, "I have sinned by betraying innocent blood."

We are told about Jesus' temptation but never about His sin. Hebrews 4:15 tells us He "has been tempted in all things as we are, yet without sin." He never had to repent or ask forgiveness.

The disciples knew Christ better than anyone else. They lived with Him in close contact for about three years. They never found in Jesus the sins they found in themselves. Peter's evaluation of Him was that He was without spot or blemish, that He committed no sin, and no deceit was found in His mouth (I Peter 1:19 and 2:22).

The apostle John was well aware of the evil in all men's hearts for he said, "If we say that we have no sin, we are deceiving ourselves and the truth is not in us" (I John 1:8). When it came to

Jesus, he said, "He appeared in order to take away sins; and in Him there is no sin" (I John 3:5. See also II Corinthians 5:21 and I Peter 3:18).

Jesus possessed a moral perfection unknown to any other person. Such a one could never have been a liar and deceiver.

Was Jesus Crazy?

Perhaps Jesus sincerely thought He was God, but was sincerely wrong. Maybe He was deluded—a lunatic. As we examine the life of Christ, we discover that He possessed all the attributes of one who had optimum mental health. He faced extreme pressure and hostile opposition with control and composure. Some of the most learned Jewish leaders tried to trap Jesus with difficult questions, yet His answers silenced and astonished His listeners (Luke 20:20-40).

Jesus spoke and acted with wisdom and authority (Matthew 7:28,29 and 13:54). His amazing and insightful teachings as well as His accurate prophecies concerning the destruction of the Temple (Matthew 24:2), fulfilled in 70 A.D., and concerning various signs of the last days (Matthew 24:4-51), reveal a supernatural insight.

Were Jesus' Miracles Genuine?

What about His miracles? Maybe they were illusions. Concerning this, Andre Kole, regarded as one of the world's foremost illusionists, stated in his book *From Illusion to Reality*:

Because of my extensive knowledge concerning the art of magic, I concluded that I might be the most qualified to determine if the miraculous events attributed to Christ could have been accomplished by trickery, or if they were indeed genuine.[24]

After extensive investigation, Andre went on to say:

>The conclusion from my study was inescapable. I could not argue with His miracles. To re-enact them as an illusionist would cost several million dollars, and it would be very obvious that they were being accomplished through stage effects. I had to agree with Nicodemus, who said to Jesus, "We know that You have come from God...for no one can do these signs [miracles] that you do unless God is with him" (John 3:2).[25]

Scripture foretold and ancient Jews believed that the Messiah would heal the sick and raise the dead. Not only would He perform miraculous physical healings, but spiritual healings as well.

When John the Baptist sent two of his disciples to ask if Jesus was the One who was to come, Jesus replied—

>Go and report to John what you have seen and heard: the blind receive sight, the lame walk, the lepers are cleansed, and the deaf hear, the dead are raised up, the poor have the Gospel preached to them (Luke 7:22).

In reference to the innumerable miracles Jesus performed, the apostle John wrote—

>Therefore many other signs Jesus also performed in the presence of the disciples, which are not written in this book; but these

have been written that you may believe that
Jesus is the Christ, the Son of God; and that
believing you may have life in His name (John
20:30,31).

The miracles Jesus performed, the lives He
made whole, and the countless people throughout
history from every background and social level
whose lives have been changed and transformed
through Him, as well as all the other undeniable
facts, indicate that truly He is the Son of God.

Some Things Can't Be Explained Away as Coincidence

The Taming of Godzilla, my personal testimony,
vividly demonstrates the transforming power of the
resurrected Christ. Additional records contained in
an upcoming book entitled, *The Impossible,* reveal
some of the miraculous accounts of how He worked
in my life and ministry after coming to know Him.

Too many amazing events have occurred since
coming to faith in Jesus Christ for me to explain
them away as mere coincidence. These incredible
accounts could also not be attributed to the power
of a positive mental attitude or visualization. Nor
was it any latent or mystical power within myself
or anyone else. Intervention by the sovereign God
of the universe is the only reasonable explanation.

It is undeniable that during Biblical times and
throughout history the God of the Bible has done
some extraordinary things in the lives of those
who walk in faith and obedience to His will. Truly
He is Lord of all.

Was the Crucifixion a Mistake?

The raising of Lazarus from the dead and numerous other miracles Jesus performed created a high intensity of expectation among the multitudes. The Jewish people were eager for the Messiah (Christ) to come and defeat the Romans and restore Israel to its former power and glory under King David. So at Jesus' triumphal entry into Jerusalem, the crowds welcomed Him with shouts of praise as they spread palm branches, and even their own garments in His path.

During His triumphal entry, Jesus rode into Jerusalem on a donkey, fulfilling Zechariah 9:9. Jesus was proclaiming Himself as king (just as I Kings 1:32-35,44 records that David had Solomon ride on his mule before having him anointed king). The people welcomed Him with shouts of Hosanna, and the words of messianic Psalm 118:26, "Blessed is the one who comes in the name of the Lord." Spreading their cloaks on the road was an act of royal homage (II Kings 9:12,13).

Less than a week after the triumphal entry, many of this same multitude were shouting for Him to be crucified. Why? What happened? They didn't understand that it was God's plan for the Christ to die during His first coming (Romans 11:25,26). Therefore, they rejected the Messiah

and called for His death. This should not be all that
surprising in light of the fact that throughout their
history, the Jews put to death many of the prophets
sent to them by God (I Kings 19:10; II Chronicles
24:20-22; Matthew 23:29-31,37; I Thessalonians
2:15...).

Numerous Old Testament Scriptures foretold
the suffering, death, and resurrection of the Messiah (Isaiah 53:5-12; Psalm 22:16; Zechariah 12:10;
Psalm 16:10). Nevertheless, the Jewish people and
their leaders, as well as Jesus' disciples, could not
understand that God's purpose was for the Christ
to first die as a sacrifice for the sins of the world.
A. B. Bruce observed, "...a crucified Christ was a
scandal and a contradiction...."[26]

Jesus foretold He was going to be crucified. It
was for this purpose He had come (John 12:27).
Mark 10:32-34 states—

> ...And again He took the twelve aside and
> began to tell them what was going to happen to
> Him, saying, "Behold, we are going up to
> Jerusalem, and the Son of Man will be delivered
> to the chief priests and the scribes; and they will
> condemn Him to death and will hand Him over
> to the Gentiles. They will mock Him and spit on
> Him, and scourge Him and kill Him, and three
> days later He will rise again."

Jesus repeatedly told His disciples He must
suffer, die, and on the third day rise again (Luke
18:31-33), but they were confused and did not
comprehend what He meant (Luke 18:34; Mark
9:9,10, 31,32).

New Testament scholar, Dr. George Eldon
Ladd, writes:

This is also why his disciples forsook him when he was taken captive. Their minds were so completely imbued with the idea of a conquering Messiah whose role it was to subdue his enemies that when they saw him broken and bleeding under the scourging, a helpless prisoner in the hands of Pilate, and when they saw him led away, nailed to a cross to die as a common criminal, all their messianic hopes for Jesus were shattered. It is a sound psychological fact that we hear only what we are prepared to hear. Jesus' predictions of his suffering and death fell on deaf ears. The disciples, in spite of his warnings, were unprepared for it, and equally unprepared for his resurrection.[27]

The Hebrew Scriptures mention a suffering servant, especially in Isaiah 53 and Psalm 22. Scripture also tells about the Messiah coming as David's heir and reigning as King. After centuries of suffering under the yoke of foreigners, and then being under Roman oppression, the Jews of first century Israel yearned for the One who would come and rule on the throne of David forever. Consequently, the Jews of Jesus' day only focused on the Messiah as coming King.

Peter actually began to rebuke Jesus for stating that He must suffer, be rejected, be killed, and rise again after three days (Mark 8:31,32). But Jesus rebuked Peter and said—

Get behind Me, Satan; for you are not setting your mind on God's interests, but man's (Mark 8:33).

The animal sacrifices in the Tanahk were a foreshadow of the death of the Messiah. Hebrews 9:22 says, "...without shedding of blood there is no forgiveness." Whereas the animal sacrifices were regular occurrences, Christ's sacrificial death was, "once...to put away sin by the sacrifice of Himself" (Hebrews 9:26).

The crucifixion of Jesus Christ was no mistake. It had been determined before the creation of the world. The Hebrew Scriptures foretold this mystery of God which was meticulously fulfilled in Jesus Christ and majestically proclaimed to both Jews and Gentiles. God's ultimate sacrifice is undeniable proof of His amazing and incomprehensible love for us.

Is There Evidence for the Resurrection?

Jesus not only foretold His crucifixion, but also claimed that He had power over life and death. He said, "I am the resurrection and the life; he who believes in Me will live even if he dies" (John 11:25).

Some have claimed that they could bodily return from the grave. Only Christ backed up His claim. Also consider that the grave of Mohammed is not an empty grave. The tomb of Confucius is not an empty tomb. Parts of Buddha's body are enshrined as relics in different places in the Orient. But there is no tomb or grave that claims Christ's body, nor is there any shrine in the world that has even one of His bones.

While working on his doctorate in philosophy and apologetics, BJ Rudge wrote an excellent article entitled, *The Resurrection: Myth or Fact?— Compelling Evidence.* Regarding how the reality of the resurrection can either validate or discredit Christianity, BJ comments:

> The apostle Paul understood the utter importance of the resurrection to a believer's faith and wrote the following to the church at Corinth, "But if there is no resurrection of the dead, not even Christ has been raised; and if

Christ has not been raised, then our preaching is vain, your faith is also in vain" (I Corinthians 15:13,14). The resurrection is part of the foundation of Christianity; without it the Christian faith will topple.

The claim that Jesus rose from the dead is not merely given on the assumption of faith, but on the grounds of historical objective testimony and evidence. As a result one must approach the resurrection on the same grounds that he would any other historical claim. He must allow the empirical evidence to determine the outcome and not his preconceived beliefs. He must be like a juror and listen to the evidence and opposing opinions then make an honest inference to the best explanation. The final decision that one makes should be based, not upon philosophical speculation, but upon one's own historical investigation of the facts.[28]

Was Jesus Dead?

Let us lay to rest the myth that Jesus really did not die on the cross or that it was faked. After all the trauma and abuse He had endured during the crucifixion ordeal, there was no way Jesus could have been alive as some skeptics have attempted to theorize. The Roman soldiers were experts in execution by crucifixion, and they knew the victims were dead before they removed them from the cross. Do some investigation into Roman scourging and crucifixion at that time, and you will be convinced that Jesus died on the cross.

There is the "swoon theory" that Jesus fainted during the crucifixion and was removed from the cross before His death.

This theory would have to say that: (1) Jesus went through six trials—three Roman and three Jewish; (2) was beaten almost beyond description by the Roman flagrum; (3) was so weak He could not carry His own *patibulum*— the wooden cross bar; (4) had spikes driven through His hands and feet as He was crucified; (5) the Romans thrust a sword into His side and eyewitnesses said, "Blood and water came out," a sign of death; (6) four executioners confirmed His death...; (7) 100-plus pounds of spices and a gummy substance were encased around His body...; (8) He was put into a cold, damp tomb; (9) a large stone was lodged against its entrance; (10) a Roman guard was stationed there, and (11) a seal was placed across the entrance.

Then an incredible thing happened, according to this theory. The cool damp air of the tomb, instead of killing Him, healed Him. He split out of His garments, pushed the stone away, fought off the guards and shortly thereafter appeared to His disciples as the Lord of life.[29]

An article dealing with the medical and historical accuracy of the physical death of Jesus Christ stated:

> The actual cause of Jesus' death...may have been multifactorial and related primarily to hypovolemic shock, exhaustion asphyxia, and perhaps acute heart failure....However, the important feature may not be *how* he died but rather *whether* he died. Clearly, the weight of historical and medical evidence indicates that Jesus was dead before the wound to his side was inflicted and supports the traditional view

that the spear, thrust between his right ribs, probably perforated not only the right lung but also the pericardium and heart and thereby ensured his death. Accordingly, interpretations based on the assumption that Jesus did not die on the cross appear to be at odds with modern medical knowledge.[30]

In his book, *The Resurrection Factor*, Josh McDowell states:

Numerous religious fears and political motives caused both the Jews and the Roman governor, Pontius Pilate, to kill Jesus Christ. To make sure He remained dead and buried, six important security precautions were taken:

1) Christ was put to death by crucifixion, one of the most effective, cruel and hideous methods of execution ever devised.

2) The body of Christ was buried in a solid rock tomb.

3) Christ's body was wrapped with more than 100 pounds of spices according to precise Jewish burial customs.

4) The stone rolled in front of the tomb entrance weighed about two tons.

5) A Roman security guard, one of the most effective fighting units devised, was positioned to guard the tomb.

6) The tomb was sealed shut with the official authority and signate of Rome.[31]

Proponents of this theory [theft of the body by disciples] would have to allege that the followers of Christ not only foisted a lie upon the people (a thought totally contrary to what their Master taught and died for) but that they lived out the rest of their lives proclaiming a lie about a "risen Christ." They would do all this as *cowards* transformed into courageous men who died as martyrs, knowing it was a deliberate fabrication.

Yet, in actuality they were willing to face arrest, imprisonment, beating, and horrible deaths, and not one of them ever denied the Lord and recanted of his belief that Christ had risen.[32]

In *More Than A Carpenter*, another insightful book by Josh McDowell, he continues to present verification for the resurrection of Jesus Christ. He states:

> The depression and cowardice of the disciples provide a hardhitting argument against their suddenly becoming so brave and daring as to face a detachment of soldiers at the tomb and steal the body. They were in no mood to attempt anything like that.[33]

McDowell continues:

> The theory that the Jewish or Roman authorities moved Christ's body is no more reasonable an explanation for the empty tomb than theft by the disciples. If the authorities had the body in their possession or knew where it was, why, when the disciples were preaching the resurrection in Jerusalem, didn't they explain that they had taken it?

If they had, why didn't they explain where the body lay? Why didn't they recover the corpse, put it on a cart, and wheel it through the center of Jerusalem? Such an action would certainly have destroyed Christianity.[34]

The Resurrection

The resurrection of Jesus Christ was preached within a few minutes' walk of Joseph's tomb. As a result of Peter's sermon proclaiming a risen Christ, 3,000 believed (Acts 2:41). Shortly thereafter, many more believed and the total reached 5,000 (Acts 4:4). Acts 4:33 states—

> And with great power the apostles were giving testimony to the resurrection of the Lord Jesus, and abundant grace was upon them all.

The result of Jesus' resurrection is also manifested in Acts 6:7—

> The word of God kept on spreading; and the number of the disciples continued to increase greatly in Jerusalem, and a great many of the priests were becoming obedient to the faith.

Before Jesus' crucifixion the disciples were thrilled by His miracles and had great expectancy for His and their future. Yet, when Jesus died at Calvary all their excitement turned into despair and their expectancy turned into hopelessness. Shortly after the crucifixion the disciples were secluded with the doors shut for fear of the Jewish authorities (John 20:19). Yet, several days later, they were so dramatically transformed that nothing or no one could silence their testimony. What happened? There is only one reasonable explanation—they saw, touched, talked to, and ate with the resurrected Christ, as well as experienced the fulfillment of His promise to send the Holy Spirit.

In Luke 24:39, Jesus said to His disciples as they were gathered in Jerusalem—

> See My hands and My feet, that it is I Myself; touch Me and see, for a spirit does not have flesh and bones as you see that I have.

It could not have been a hallucination, for Jesus was seen on more than a dozen occasions recorded in the New Testament, at one time before 500 eyewitnesses—most of whom were alive at the time the account was recorded in Scripture (I Corinthians 15:6). People from different backgrounds and in different circumstances, most of whom had no expectancy of seeing Him and some of whom actually ate with Him and touched Him, testified of His resurrection.

These same disciples were soon on trial in Jerusalem, the city where Jesus was crucified, and stood before the very ones responsible for their leader's death. Neither beatings, nor threats of persecution, imprisonment, or death could quiet them. They said when threatened, "We cannot stop speaking about what we have seen and heard" (Acts 4:20).

Peter, who cowered in fear the night before the crucifixion because a servant girl asked him if he was a disciple of Jesus, was so transformed that just a few weeks later he boldly witnessed before thousands of people concerning Christ's resurrection, and eventually gave his life as a martyr. It has been pointedly asked, "If the disciples had deceitfully attempted to start a new faith, would they have given their lives for such a lie?"

The only possible explanation for the transformation is this—

He [Jesus] presented Himself alive after His
suffering, by many convincing proofs, appearing
to them [the apostles] over a period of forty days
(Acts 1:3).

Concerning Jesus being seen by His disciples
following His resurrection, doctoral student BJ
Rudge states:

The final evidential proof to be looked at is
the postmortem appearances. In the Gospels
there are numerous accounts of eyewitnesses
who testify that Jesus appeared to them after
His death. Many theories have been proposed
to explain these appearances. Before looking
at them there are a few key points that need to
be made about these appearances. First, these
appearances were not secluded to a few
people, but to a vast number of people from
different geographical locations. The apostle
Paul says that Jesus appeared to over 500
people, "...and that He appeared to Cephas,
then to the twelve. After that He appeared to
more than five hundred brethren at one
time...then He appeared to James, then to all
the apostles; and last of all,...He appeared to
me also" (I Corinthians 15:5-8).

Secondly, these appearances were not of
the same manner. For example, Jesus
appeared to Mary Magdalene outside the tomb,
while on another occasion He appeared to
Thomas with the other disciples behind closed

doors. Third, these appearances brought about different responses from those who saw Jesus. Mary Magdalene responded in joy as she clung to Jesus, while in other appearances people responded in fright thinking they had seen a spirit. The fact that the appearances cannot be harmonized gives credence to the idea that they were not fabricated. Fourth, the resurrection appearances are reported without mystical and fanciful descriptions. Fifth, the witnesses testified to these appearances in spite of Jesus' enemies being present. Finally, these appearances immediately changed the lives of the disciples (and others) to the extent that they were willing to give up their lives. The disciples extraordinarily changed from men of fear and doubt to men of boldness and courage as they openly proclaimed the resurrection of Jesus Christ.[35]

Changed Lives

In his book *Who Moved the Stone?*, Frank Morison comments:

First, it is undeniable that, despite his earlier and unfeigned hostility, James, the brother of Jesus, did go over to the church and that, upon the authority of Josephus, he perished violently on its behalf.[36]

Wilbur M. Smith writes in *Therefore Stand:*

That it was faith in the Resurrection of Christ, and the preaching of this stupendous truth, that gave the early church its power to win thousands and then millions of idolatrous

citizens of the great Roman Empire for Christ,
though vast multitudes of them in confessing
their faith knew they were dooming themselves
to torture and social ostracism, is recognized
among all who have given any careful
consideration to the intricate, difficult
problems of the establishment of the Christian
church in the Roman world.[37]

According to Biblical researcher Jim Weikal, it
is amazing that by 64 A.D., Christianity had
impacted Rome so extensively that the evil Roman
Emperor Nero used Christians as scapegoats for
his own infamous actions. Tacitus (c.A.D. 55 -
c.120), a pagan historian and no friend of
Christianity, writes of the intense and diabolical
tortures during the reign of this madman:

> Nero...inflicted the most exquisite tortures
> on a class hated for their abominations, called
> Christians by the populace. Christus, from
> whom the name had its origin, suffered the
> extreme penalty during the reign of Tiberius at
> the hands of one of our procurators, Pontius
> Pilatus.... Mockery of every sort was added to
> their [the Christians'] deaths. Covered with the
> skins of beasts, they were torn by dogs and
> perished, or were nailed to crosses, or were
> doomed to the flames and burnt, to serve as a
> nightly illumination, when daylight had
> expired.[38]

During early church history, many believers
were subjected to public humiliation, tortured,
thrown to wild animals, burned at the stake,
crucified, and beheaded because they refused to

deny the reality of the resurrected Christ. The apostles were no exception:

> All except one of the original apostles died a martyr's death for witnessing to the deity of Christ. Throughout history, people have willingly died for a lie when they did not know it was a lie. But it is contrary to all human experience for a group of men to die as martyrs, claiming that a lie was the truth when they knew differently.[39]

Jesus appeared to the apostle John on the Isle of Patmos more than half a century after His resurrection. He spoke these memorable words: "I was dead, and behold, I am alive forevermore" (Revelation 1:18).

Saul of Tarsus was a zealous Jew—a Pharisee—who severely persecuted the early Christian church and was involved with the stoning of Stephen. However, in Acts 9 we read of a miracle that occurred in which he had an encounter with the resurrected Christ.

As a result of his dramatic conversion, Saul of Tarsus, later known as Paul the apostle, became one of the strongest spokesmen for the resurrection, earnestly and effectively explaining from the Hebrew Scriptures that Jesus was the Messiah (Acts 28:23). He wrote much of the New Testament, testified before both Jewish and Roman authorities, endured beatings, stonings, imprisonments, suffered hardships too numerous to mention, and eventual martyrdom—all for the cause of Christ Jesus.

Two professors at Oxford, the eminent Gilbert West and Lord Lyttelton, the famous English jurist, were determined to destroy Christianity. But to do so, both of these avowed skeptics agreed that two things were necessary. They must disprove the resurrection, and they must dispose of the conversion of the apostle Paul. They divided the task between them, West assuming responsibility for proving the fallacy of the resurrection and Lyttelton disproving Paul's conversion on the Damascus road. They were to give themselves plenty of time— a year or more if necessary. When they met again to compare notes, they both had become strong and devoted Christians, each testifying to the remarkable change in his life through contact with the risen Christ.

Frank Morison, an English journalist, set out to prove that the story of Christ's resurrection was a myth. However, he ended up writing a book entitled, *Who Moved The Stone?*, in which he sets forth the truthfulness of the resurrection.

As a pre-law student, Josh McDowell had initially set out to refute Christianity, but after extensive research, became a committed believer. He has since written several books on the evidence of the resurrection and the validity of the Christian faith.

Countless others throughout history have discovered the reality of God's promise that the Messiah would be "a light of the nations so that My salvation may reach to the end of the earth" (Isaiah 49:6).

We have just skimmed the surface of the awesome and overwhelming evidence for the resurrection of Jesus Christ. The depth and riches of God's wisdom and love are incomparable. Jesus resurrection is confirming proof that He is the Messiah of the Jews and the Savior of the world.

A Wise Decision

Without a doubt, Jesus of Nazareth is the most unique individual who ever lived. No one before and no one after Him has influenced history as greatly as He has. This alone should motivate anyone to want to know more about Him.

Jesus stands high above all the world's greatest religious leaders in a category all by Himself. There is unsurpassed proof that He is the promised Messiah, the only way of salvation, and uniquely God incarnate.

Acceptance of Jesus Christ as Savior and Lord, therefore, is not a blind leap of faith in the dark, but a very wise and reasonable decision. Check out the facts for yourself. They speak loud and clear. The evidence is compelling. His credibility is sound. His claims are true.

John 20:31—

> ...but these have been written so that you may believe that Jesus is the Christ, the Son of God; and that believing you may have life in His name.

Those who refuse to make their lives accountable to the God who created them have no alternative but to make up theories and to deny Him. But those who come with an open heart, sincerely seeking the God of the Bible, will find Him.

The More I Searched

People used to tell me that being a Christian is foolish and weak. Now I know that is a lie. The wisest decision I ever made was to give my life to Jesus Christ. I have lived the other lifestyles, and I assure you it takes far more courage and strength to live totally for the Lord.

Before I became a Christian I investigated many other religions and philosophies. Although sincere in their beliefs and having some truth, they did not have sufficient evidence to convince and motivate me to commit my life.

I have served and walked with the Lord Jesus Christ since 1971. He has proven faithful and true. As stated before, I did not accept Jesus Christ because I needed Him or because my life was all messed up. The more I searched and the more I researched, the more I became convinced that He is who He claimed to be.

No one has been able to show me a religious philosophy with more wisdom and accuracy than Biblical Christianity. No religious philosophy in the world has more historical, archeological, scientific, and prophetic evidence than what is found in the Bible.

The next time someone asks you, "Where do I find truth?," you can answer with confidence, "In Jesus Christ!" You can stand up unashamedly for your faith in Him and your belief in the validity of Scripture.

Will Jesus Return?

I am convinced from many years of prophetic research that Jesus will return (Acts 1:10,11), and then the following prophecy will be fulfilled—

Every knee will bow...and every tongue will confess that Jesus Christ is Lord, to the glory of God the Father (Philippians 2:10,11).

According to Scripture, no one will have to wonder at the Second Coming of Jesus Christ. Revelation 1:7 says—

Behold, He is coming with the clouds, and every eye will see Him, even those who pierced Him; and all the tribes of the earth will mourn over Him.

In Acts 1:11, as Jesus ascended into heaven, two angels said to His disciples—

Men of Galilee, why do you stand looking into the sky? This Jesus, who has been taken up from you into heaven, will come in just the same way as you have watched Him go into heaven.

Matthew 24:27-31 says—

For just as the lightning comes from the
east and flashes even to the west, so will the
coming of the Son of Man be...and then the sign
of the Son of Man will appear in the sky, and
then all the tribes of the earth will mourn, and
they will see the Son of Man coming on the
clouds of the sky with power and great glory.
And He will send forth His angels with a great
trumpet and they will gather together His elect
from the four winds, from one end of the sky to
the other.

Daniel 7:13,14 says—

I kept looking in the night visions, and
behold, with the clouds of heaven One like a
Son of Man was coming, and He came up to the
Ancient of Days and was presented before Him.
And to Him was given dominion, glory and a
kingdom, that all the peoples, nations, and men
of every language might serve Him. His
dominion is an everlasting dominion which will
not pass away; and His kingdom is one which
will not be destroyed.

We Will Be Transformed

I Corinthians 15:51,52 reveals that when Jesus
Christ returns believers will be transformed. It
says—

Behold, I tell you a mystery; we will not all
sleep, but we will all be changed, in a moment,
in the twinkling of an eye....

I Thessalonians 4:16-18 states—

For the Lord Himself will descend from heaven with a shout, with the voice of the archangel and with the trumpet of God, and the dead in Christ will rise first. Then we who are alive and remain will be caught up together with them in the clouds to meet the Lord in the air, and so we shall always be with the Lord. Therefore comfort one another with these words.

At His Second Coming, the Biblical evidence, cataclysmic signs, and physical transformation of believers will undeniably confirm Him to be the true Messiah.

How You Can Know Him

Christ's disciples were first called Christians at Antioch (Acts 11:26). Its original meaning was that of servants and followers of Jesus Christ. Today, this term has a much broader and oftentimes entirely different meaning than its initial use. It has become one of the most misunderstood words in our language.

Many believe that a Christian is someone who merely goes to church, believes in God, lives a good life, or tries to keep the commandments. While it is true that such things as joining a church, water baptism, living a godly lifestyle, and a loving attitude should definitely be marks of a believer, these should never be misconstrued as being the criteria for someone becoming a Christian. We must examine Scripture and, based upon its authority, determine what it really means to come to faith in Jesus Christ.

Not by Works

According to Scripture, doing good works or keeping God's Law does not make anyone a Christian. The apostle Paul explains that one of the purposes of the Law in the Tanakh (Old Testament), which is based upon the Ten Commandments, was to show us that we all are sinners and can never achieve the standards required by God. Because of our sinful nature, we continually fall short of the mark. This dilemma reveals our need for a Savior—

> By the works of the Law no flesh will be justified in His sight; for through the Law comes the knowledge of sin (Romans 3:20).
>
> Therefore the Law has become our tutor to lead us to Christ, so that we may be justified by faith (Galatians 3:24).
>
> Therefore they said to Him, "What shall we do, so that we may work the works of God?" Jesus answered and said to them, "This is the work of God, that you believe in Him whom He has sent" (John 6:28,29).

Paul makes it clear that God's righteousness can only be obtained through faith, and that Israel did not attain it because they sought it not by faith, but by works. He states—

> What then shall we say? That the Gentiles, who did not pursue righteousness, have obtained it, a righteousness that is by faith; but Israel, who pursued a law of righteousness, has not attained it.
>
> Why not? Because they pursued it not by faith but as if it were by works. They stumbled over the "stumbling stone."
>
> As it is written: "See, I lay in Zion a stone that causes men to stumble and a rock that makes them fall, and the one who trusts in Him will never be put to shame" (Romans 9:30-33 NIV).

By Faith

It is by faith in Jesus Christ, therefore, that we are saved. He is the stone mentioned in the above passage. Those who reject Him stumble and fall; those who trust in Him are saved.

II Timothy 1:9—

[God] who has saved us and called us with a holy calling, not according to our works, but according to His own purpose and grace which was granted us in Christ Jesus from all eternity.

Titus 3:4-7—

But when the kindness of God our Savior and His love for mankind appeared, He saved us, not on the basis of deeds which we have done in righteousness, but according to His mercy, by the washing of regeneration and renewing by the Holy Spirit, whom He poured out upon us richly through Jesus Christ our Savior, so that being justified by His grace we would be made heirs according to the hope of eternal life.

Nothing is more tragic than someone pursuing a false hope of salvation through his or her own works and self-effort when Jesus offers true salvation as a free gift. The apostle Paul writes—

For by grace you have been saved through faith; and that not of yourselves, it is the gift of God; not as a result of works, so that no one may boast (Ephesians 2:8,9).

We maintain that a man is justified by faith apart from works of the Law (Romans 3:28).

We know that a man is not justified by observing the Law, but by faith in Jesus Christ. So we, too, have put our faith in Christ Jesus that we may be justified by faith in Christ and not by observing the Law, because by observing the Law no one will be justified (Galatians 2:16 NIV).

For I testify about them that they have a zeal for God, but not in accordance with knowledge. For not knowing about God's righteousness and seeking to establish their own, they did not subject themselves to the righteousness of God. For Christ is the end of the Law for righteousness to everyone who believes (Romans 10:2-4).

Only through the shed blood of Jesus Christ is forgiveness available and a restored relationship with the Father made possible. Only Christ is the perfect sacrifice and substitute that satisfied a holy and just God.

II Corinthians 5:21—

He made Him who knew no sin to be sin on our behalf, so that we might become the righteousness of God in Him.

Colossians 1:22—

He has now reconciled you in His fleshly body through death, in order to present you before Him holy and blameless and beyond reproach.

Although we are all guilty of sin and rebellion, when we put our faith in Jesus Christ, His perfect righteousness is applied to our lives. We become acceptable to God solely through faith in Christ's

sacrificial death—"without shedding of blood
there is no forgiveness" (Hebrews 9:22). The
animal sacrifices in the Hebrew Scriptures were
merely a foreshadowing of the death of God's Son
on the cross.

> For Christ died for sins once for all, the
> righteous for the unrighteous, to bring you to
> God (I Peter 3:18 NIV).

Jesus paid the penalty for our sins. He suffered
and died in our place. We don't have to "perform" for
God out of fear and guilt, but are now free to serve
and obey Him because we know and love Him.

That is why the apostle Paul could so boldly
say—

> If anyone else has a mind to put confidence
> in the flesh, I far more: circumcised the eighth
> day, of the nation of Israel, of the tribe of
> Benjamin, a Hebrew of Hebrews; as to the Law,
> a Pharisee; as to zeal, a persecutor of the
> church; as to the righteousness which is in the
> Law, found blameless. But whatever things
> were gain to me, those things I have counted as
> loss for the sake of Christ. More than that, I
> count all things to be loss in view of the
> surpassing value of knowing Christ Jesus my
> Lord, for whom I have suffered the loss of all
> things, and count them but rubbish so that I
> may gain Christ, and may be found in Him, not
> having a righteousness of my own derived from
> the Law, but that which is through faith in
> Christ, the righteousness which comes from
> God on the basis of faith (Philippians 3:4-9).

Paul also said in Acts 20:24—

But I do not consider my life of any account
as dear to myself, so that I may finish my course
and the ministry which I received from the Lord
Jesus, to testify solemnly of the gospel of the
grace of God.

Faith and Works

Good works done after accepting Christ stem
from a heart of gratitude. Thankful for what the
Lord accomplished on the cross, a believer does
good deeds, but these acts are only the *fruit* and
result of salvation, not the *cause for* it.

Paul emphasizes that we are not justified by
moral and ceremonial acts performed in obedience
to the Law, but through faith in Christ. James,
however, places emphasis on the resultant good
works that flow out of true Biblical faith. He stresses
that we are not justified merely by a barren
orthodoxy—which even the demons possess and
shudder (James 2:19), but by true faith that
produces works (James 2:14-26).

Paul and James are in agreement. Paul concurs
that the faith which saves ultimately results in good
works—"deeds appropriate to repentance" (Acts
26:20; see also Ephesians 2:8-10).

The Bible is therefore clear. We are not saved
by dead faith (James 2:17) nor by dead works
(Hebrews 6:1; 9:14), but by a living faith which
results in "love and good deeds" (Hebrews 10:24).

In summary, the apostle Paul tells us we are
saved totally by faith and as a result of that saving
faith, good works follow. James agrees that the
proof of saving faith is works of righteousness.

Works flow out of one's inner heart—one's
nature, and that nature can only be changed by

God's grace. The new birth is a work from above—
not the work of man (John 1:12,13).

An interesting account in the Gospels tells of
Zacchaeus, a chief tax collector, welcoming Jesus
to his home—an act of faith and acceptance.
Zacchaeus then shows the fruit of faith by
promising to give half his possessions to the poor
and paying back fourfold anyone he had cheated.
Jesus said to him—

> Today salvation has come to this house....
> For the Son of Man has come to seek and to save
> that which was lost (Luke 19:9,10).

There is a delicate balance between grace and
obedience:

> Works are the unmistakable evidence of
> the loyalty of the heart; they express either
> belief or unbelief, faithfulness or unfaithful-
> ness. The judgment [Revelation 20:11-15] will
> reveal whether or not one's loyalties were with
> God and the Lamb or with God's enemies.[40]

God's Righteousness

We cannot expect to be accepted by God because
of our own goodness. Romans 3:23 points this out
emphatically: "for all have sinned and fall short of
the glory of God." This does not mean that we
cannot do good, but according to God's standard of
righteousness, we all miss the mark.

In all the religions of the world, there are people
seeking to establish their own righteousness to
earn salvation. In Biblical Christianity, however, it
is the righteousness of Jesus Christ which makes
possible salvation as a free gift through faith to
those who will receive it.

I am not ashamed of the gospel, because it is the power of God for the salvation of everyone who believes.... For in the gospel a righteousness from God is revealed, a righteousness that is by faith from first to last, just as it is written: "The righteous will live by faith" (Romans 1:16,17 NIV).

The Hebrew Scriptures state concerning Abraham—

Then he believed in the Lord; and He reckoned it to him as righteousness (Genesis 15:6).

See Romans chapter four for additional insight on Abraham being justified by faith.

Not a Religion

The world is filled with various religions, but salvation is found only in Jesus Christ. Scripture tells us—

And there is salvation in no one else; for there is no other name under heaven that has been given among men by which we must be saved (Acts 4:12).

Religion is one's attempt to worship God with man-made traditions and ideas, but true faith is one's belief and love for God through His Son Jesus Christ. Religion is what one does for his God, but salvation is what God has done for us—

...that God was reconciling the world to Himself in Christ, not counting men's sins against them (II Corinthians 5:19 NIV).

Jesus Christ is God's unique revelation of salvation. This is why Jesus (as recorded in the Gospel of John) could honestly say—

I am the way, and the truth, and the life; no one comes to the Father but through Me (John 14:6).

Some people have just enough religion to make them miserable. While they know the "language" and go through all the "motions," they have never known the joy and peace of having a real and personal relationship with Jesus Christ. Nobody is more miserable than the person trying to be a Christian in his or her own strength. Many have, therefore, turned away and rejected what they thought was Christianity, but in truth is not.

A Relationship

A person I knew had attended church all his life but was never taught that he could know Christ in a real and personal way. Being disillusioned with what he thought was Christianity, he began searching for answers in Eastern religions. He felt God was impersonal and unknowable. I showed him numerous Scriptures that proved to him that God does want us to know Him and have a personal relationship with Him. God's Word helped clarify for him the true meaning of being a Christian. He realized that this was what he had always longed for.

Know the Lord

I shared the following illustration with a couple—the husband had cancer and didn't have much time to live—who were religious, knowing about God, but they didn't know the Lord in a personal way. I said, "If a stranger would walk in your front door and say, 'Hi, I'm home! I'm going up to my room,' you would respond by quickly saying, 'I don't know who you are. Get out of here!' However, if one of your own children walked in and said the same thing, you'd say, 'Glad to see you! Come on in!' "

In the Bible, Jesus said there will be those who think that they are His children because they go to church or profess to believe in Him, but when they stand before Him, He will in essence say, "Get out of here. I never knew you— you're not My child" (Matthew 7:21-23). In contrast, Jesus will say to those He knows, "I know you. You're mine—enter into the joy of your Lord."

I assured them that we can know now what type of greeting we will receive when we meet the Lord. I shared the words of Paul in II Timothy 1:12, "....I know Whom I have believed and I am convinced that He is able to guard what I have entrusted to Him until that day."

While I was buying blueberries, the young lady selling them told me about the recent death of her father. She was still grieving, so I asked her if her father knew the Lord. I wanted to find out her perspective in an attempt to bring her some hope and encouragement. She said, "Yes, he made his peace with God." I asked, "How about you?" She informed me she went to church but wasn't close to the Lord.

I said to her, "You can tell me about your father and even show me pictures, and although I can know all about him, I will never have a personal relationship with him like you had." I continued, "Most people who go to church know about God like I would about your father, but God wants us to know Him in a personal way as you knew your father." Her eyes lit up as she told me that this is what she longed for.

After prayer, she hugged me as tears streamed down her face. She said, "This was not a chance meeting; I was meant to talk to you."

It is interesting to note that the Greek word for "know" *(ginosko)*, used when Jesus said, "I never knew you; depart from Me ..." (Matthew 7:23) is the very same word used for "know," which was used by Mary when she said to the angel Gabriel, who had come to announce the birth of Jesus, "How shall this be, seeing I know not a man?" (Luke 1:34 KJV) She never had an intimate relationship with a man. The same Greek word for "know" was used again when Jesus said—

> This is eternal life, that they may know You, the only true God, and Jesus Christ whom You have sent (John 17:3).

Scripture teaches that we must *know* the Lord by having an intimate and personal relationship with Jesus Christ. A Christian is someone who has a restored relationship with God the Father through a personal faith and acceptance of His Son Jesus and His finished work on the cross. The true concept of Biblical Christianity is not a lifeless external form of religion, but a living vital personal relationship with the Creator of the universe who is knowable and seeks to be known.

New Lordship

Before I became a Christian, I was my own god, running my life my own way. I didn't want anybody, including God, telling me what to do. When I came to faith in Jesus Christ, however, I submitted to His Lordship. The throne of my life has now been restored to its rightful King. Rebellion and pride used to separate me from God. The peace I now have with God has been made possible by His own provision—His Son Jesus Christ. Romans 5:1 puts it this way—

> Therefore, having been justified by faith, we have peace with God through our Lord Jesus Christ.

To be justified means to be declared righteous. God now forgives us and accepts us because of the imputed righteousness of Christ. His righteousness, in effect, becomes our righteousness.

The qualifying factor for us to receive God's forgiveness and to be declared righteous by Him is that we "believe in" the Lord Jesus Christ. Following an amazing chain of events, the Philippian jailer asked Paul and Silas, "Sirs, what must I do to be saved?" They said, "Believe in the Lord Jesus, and you will be saved" (Acts 16:30,31).

Romans 10:9,10 states—

> ...that if you confess with your mouth Jesus as Lord, and believe in your heart that God raised Him from the dead, you will be saved; for with the heart a person believes, resulting in righteousness, and with the mouth he confesses, resulting in salvation.

A Greek word study will reveal that to "believe in" means to be persuaded of, and hence, to trust in, rely on, and be faithful to. To "believe in" is not merely acknowledging the reality of Christ, but a *belief* that results in your accepting His free gift of salvation, having confidence in Him as the only way of salvation, and thereby committing your life to Him. It means to persevere in trust and obedience.

John 1:12—

But as many as received Him, to them He gave the right to become children of God, even to those who believe in His name.

Feelings

When you give your life to Christ, the feelings may or may not be there, but the fact remains— you are now forgiven and beginning a new life in Christ. Feelings are merely an emotional response as you realize and appreciate what God has done for you in Jesus Christ and what the Holy Spirit has begun in your life.

If you obtain a marriage license and get married, you may or may not feel differently. It doesn't matter how you feel. The fact is that you are now married. It's the same with God. By faith one receives God's forgiveness and restoration in Christ, and according to God's Word, a new life and relationship begins.

I John 5:11,12—

And the testimony is this, that God has given us eternal life, and this life is in His Son. He who has the Son has the life; he who does not have the Son of God does not have the life.

New Creation

Jesus said to Nicodemus in John 3:3—

Truly, truly, I say to you, unless one is born again he cannot see the kingdom of God.

Jesus informed Nicodemus, a Pharisee and member of the Sanhedrin, that one could not see or enter the Kingdom of God without spiritual rebirth. One must be "born again" or "born from above."

Ephesians 2:4,5 states—

But God, being rich in mercy, because of His great love with which He loved us, even when we were dead in our transgressions, made us alive together with Christ (by grace you have been saved).

II Corinthians 5:17 says—

Therefore if anyone is in Christ, he is a new creature; the old things passed away; behold, new things have come.

This does not mean that once we accept Christ, we become perfect and no longer sin, but it does mean that our attitude of rebellion and self-centeredness begins to change to obedience and Christ-centeredness. We begin growing and maturing in this new life as we develop a whole new way of thinking and acting.

As we yield and submit to Jesus Christ through obedience to His Word and Spirit, He begins to mold and develop our lives. As we make our lives available to Him so He can work in and through us, we are enabled to begin fulfilling God's ultimate goal for our lives—being conformed to the image of His Son (Romans 8:29; II Corinthians 3:18).

How good it is to know that our new birth is only the beginning of our new relationship with the Lord and the beginning of a continual growth process in our new life. You now have the assurance from Scripture that God "is at work in you, both to will and to work for His good pleasure" (Philippians 2:13), and that "He who began a good work in you will carry it on to completion until the day of Christ Jesus" (Philippians 1:6 NIV).

Is Your Name in the Book of Life?

This world is not all that there is to life. Jesus Christ will return as the victorious King and Judge of the world. Those who have rejected God's provision of salvation—Jesus Christ, the Lamb of God—will be eternally separated from God's presence where there will be "weeping and gnashing of teeth." Those who have believed in the Lord Jesus Christ for salvation will receive glorified bodies and rule and reign with Him for eternity.

John 5:24 promises—

Truly, truly, I say to you, he who hears My word, and believes Him who sent Me, has eternal life, and does not come into judgment, but has passed out of death into life.

Have you committed your life to Jesus Christ? Is your name written in the Book of Life? If you do not willingly make Him Lord of your life now, you will suffer the eternal consequences.

Revelation 21:27 emphatically states—

and nothing unclean...shall ever come into it [God's Holy City], but only those whose names are written in the Lamb's book of life.

Revelation 20:15 strongly warns—

> And if anyone's name was not found written
> in the book of life, he was thrown into the lake
> of fire.

Experience His Reality

Years ago, by God's grace, I chose to commit
my life to Jesus Christ. Making a 180-degree turn,
I began following Him as Savior and Lord. It's
called repentance—dying to self and living for
Christ. I asked His forgiveness for my life of
rebellion and sin and acknowledged His rightful
position as Lord of my life. I obeyed His Word by
being baptized, and developed a consistent life of
Bible study, prayer, and fellowship with other
Biblical Christians. I strive to live for the Lord
with all my heart, with all my mind, and with all
my strength.

You, too, can have new life in Christ. Repent
and believe in the Lord Jesus. As one whose name
is written in the Lamb's Book of Life, you will
inherit all that God has prepared for those who
love Him and obey His Word. Once you experience
a life-changing faith in Jesus Christ, you will want
to grow in Him and begin uncovering the depths
of the treasures of wisdom and knowledge in Him
and His Word.

How you answer the questions, "Who is this
Jesus?" and "How can I know Him?," is eternally
significant.

John 3:16—

> For God so loved the world, that He gave His
> only begotten Son, that whoever believes in Him
> shall not perish, but have eternal life.

I do hope you will join me and the millions of others throughout history whose lives have been dramatically changed through the transforming power of the resurrected Christ. Surrender your life to Him today. Experience His peace and joy that transcends your circumstances—and have hope for the life to come. Coming to know Him as Savior and Lord will be the wisest and most courageous decision you will ever make. Living fully for Him is the most exciting, challenging, and fulfilling lifestyle available.

Footnotes

1. Herbert Lockyer, *All the Messianic Prophesies of the Bible*, Zondervan Publishing House, Grand Rapids, MI, 1973, p. 523.
2. Fred John Meldau, *Messiah in Both Testaments,* The Christian Victory Publishing Company, Denver, CO, 1956, pp. 34-35.
3. *Ibid.*, p. 25.
4. Mark Eastman and Chuck Smith, *The Search for Messiah,* Joy Publishing, Fountain Valley, CA/The Word for Today, Costa Mesa, CA, 1996, pp. 104, 110.
5. Rachmiel Frydland, *What the Rabbis Know About the Messiah,* Messianic Publishing Company, Cincinnati, OH, 1993, pp. 74-76.
6. *Ibid.*, pp. 76, 77.
7. Douglas Bookman, "Confirmation of Jesus' Messiahship", *Israel My Glory* magazine, January/ February 2002, p. 17
8. D. Guthrie, J.A. Motyer, eds., *The Eerdmans Bible Commentary—Third Edition*, WM. B. Eerdmans Publishing Company, Grand Rapids, MI, 1989, p. 465.
9. Adam Clarke, "Isaiah 53," *Commentary on the Holy Bible*, Baker Book House, Grand Rapids, MI, 1971, p. 603.
10. *The Search for Messiah,* p. 34.
11. Charles F. Pfeiffer, Howard F. Vos, John Rea, eds., *Wycliffe Bible Dictionary,* Hendrickson Publishers, Peabody, MA, 1998, p. 1110.
12. *The Search for Messiah,* pp. 119, 59, 135.

13. Willem A. VanGemeren, ed., *New International Dictionary of Old Testament Theology and Exegesis, Vol. 2*, Zondervan Publishing House, Grand Rapids, MI, 1997, p. 1126.

14. Robert Morey, *The Trinity: Evidence and Issues*, World Publishing, Grand Rapids, MI, 1996, p. 211.

15. *The Search for Messiah*, pp. 198, 199.

16. Josh McDowell, *Answers to Tough Questions*, Here's Life Publishers, San Bernardino, CA, 1983, p. 39.

17. *Messiah in Both Testaments*, p. 86.

18. *The Trinity: Evidence and Issues*, p. 301.

19. *Ibid*, p. 377.

20. J.I. Packer, Merrill C. Tenney, and William White, Jr., "Jesus Christ," *Nelson's Illustrated Encyclopedia of Bible Facts*, Thomas Nelson Publishers, Nashville, TN, 1995, p. 526.

21. *The Trinity: Evidence and Issues*, pp. 106, 362.

22. Colin Brown, ed., *The New International Dictionary of New Testament Theology*, Vol. 3, Zondervan Publishing House, Grand Rapids, MI, 1986, p. 718.

23. *Who Do You Say That I Am?*, pamphlet reprinted from *Cornerstone*, JPUSA Productions, Chicago, IL, 1979.

24. Andre Kole and Al Janssen, *From Illusion to Reality*, Here's Life Publishers, Inc., San Bernardino, CA, 1984, p. 91.

25. *Ibid.*, p. 99.

26. A. B. Bruce, *The Training of the Twelve*, Kregel Publications, Grand Rapids, MI, 1971, p. 177.

27. George Eldon Ladd, *I Believe in the Resurrection of Jesus*, William B. Eerdmans Publishing Company, Grand Rapids, MI, 1975, p. 38.

28. BJ Rudge, *The Resurrection: Myth or Fact?—Compelling Evidence*, Bill Rudge Ministries newsletter, Volume 23, Number 9, April 2001.

29. Josh McDowell, *The Resurrection Factor*, Here's Life Publishers, Inc., San Bernardino, CA, 1981, p. 98.

30. William D. Edwards, Wesley J. Gabel, Floyd E. Hosmer, *On the Physical Death of Jesus Christ*, JAMA, Vol. 255, No. 11, March 21, 1986, p. 1463.

31. *The Resurrection Factor*, p. 61.

32. *Ibid.*, p. 94.

33. Josh McDowell, *More Than A Carpenter,* Tyndale House Publishers, Carol Stream, IL, p. 95.

34. *Ibid.,* pp. 95-96.

35. *The Resurrection: Myth or Fact?—Compelling Evidence.*

36. Frank Morison, *Who Moved the Stone?,* Zondervan Publishing House, Grand Rapids, MI, 1958, p. 192.

37. Wilbur M. Smith, *Therefore Stand,* Kregel Publications, Grand Rapids, MI, pp. 367-368.

38. Moses Hadas, ed., *The Complete Works of Tacitus*, Book XV:44, Alfred John Church and William Jackson Brodribb, trans., Random House, N.Y., 1942, pp. 380-381.

39. *From Illusion to Reality,* pp. 93-94.

40. Kenneth L. Barker and John R. Kohlenberger III, eds., *Zondervan NIV Bible Commentary: Vol. 2, New Testament,* Zondervan Publishing House, Grand Rapids, MI, 1994, p. 1223.

FOR MORE INFORMATION:

Bill Rudge has produced numerous books, pamphlets, and cassettes on a variety of other timely topics. For a complete listing and a copy of his informative newsletter, write to:

Bill Rudge Ministries
P.O. Box 108
Sharon, PA 16146-0108
USA

www.billrudge.org